Dedicated to souls seeking peace when within the storm, and to finding strength in moments of stillness.

May this book be a guide to inner calm and resilience, helping illuminate a path to serenity, balance, and authenticity.

Copyright (c) 2024 Tanya Clark
Published by Ynqyry Publishing,
an imprint of YNQYRY Pty Ltd, www.ynqyry.com.

All rights reserved. No part of this publication may be reproduced, distributed, stored in a retrieval system or transmitted by any form in any means, electronic, mechanical, photocopying, recording or otherwise, without the prior written permission of the publisher and copyright holders.
No AI Training: Without in any way limiting the author's and publisher's exclusive rights under copyright, any use of this publication to "train" generative artificial intelligence (AI) technologies to generate text is expressly prohibited.

ISBN: 978-1-923280-01-4 (ebook)
ISBN: 978-1-923280-00-7 (paperback)
ISBN: 978-1-923280-02-1 (hardcover)

Being - Balance & Authenticity
A Visual Meditation Collection
Being Restful - Ebb and Flow (Series 1, Volume 1)

Being
– Balance & Authenticity
A Visual Meditation Collection

Invite mindfulness, intention, and self-inquiry into your life.

Scientific research is showing that meditation beneficially enhances our mental and physical wellbeing, and that by integrating mindful awareness and gratitude into our daily lives we are able to better cultivate inner peace, empowerment, and happiness.

Guided imagery meditation is a mindfulness practice that can be used for relaxation and wellbeing.

It involves focusing your attention on positive images and thoughts in order to achieve a state of calm and relaxation.

This series has been developed as short, visual guides to help you step into a state of calm and peaceful presence.

About Being

— Balance & Authenticity

A Visual Meditation Collection

Introducing a collection of short visual meditations designed to invoke a tranquil oasis in the chaos of everyday life.

These volumes are your passport to inner serenity, carefully crafted to empower you through moments of self-reflection and rejuvenation.

Each volume offers a gentle escape, allowing you to effortlessly dip in and out as you need, wherever and whenever.

Whether you are seeking solace during a hectic day, longing for a peaceful respite amidst life's challenges, or simply craving a moment of stillness, these meditations can become cherished companions on the path to tranquility.

Being Restful

When you have a few minutes or perhaps a leisurely afternoon, this Being Restful Collection can be a beautiful companion, guiding you to a serene space where you can reconnect with your essence and find peace in the present moment.

Ebb and Flow

Allow this meditation to guide you to a place of deep relaxation where the soothing essence of rest brings renewal, healing, and connection.

To begin, settle into a comfortable position.

Today, you will be connecting your breath with the ebb and flow of ocean waves.

Imagine you are seated, relaxing on a beach.

The water and sky are summer blue.

The sun is overhead,
its rays warm your skin,
your flesh, your muscles,
your very essence.

A cooling sea breeze glides smoothly over — and all around you.

Exhale, releasing any tension.

Waves break against the shore.

Puffy, voluminous white clouds float by overhead.

You are seated on a soft,
fluffy beach towel.
The sun is warm.
The temperature is perfect.

Children are laughing and playing in the distance.

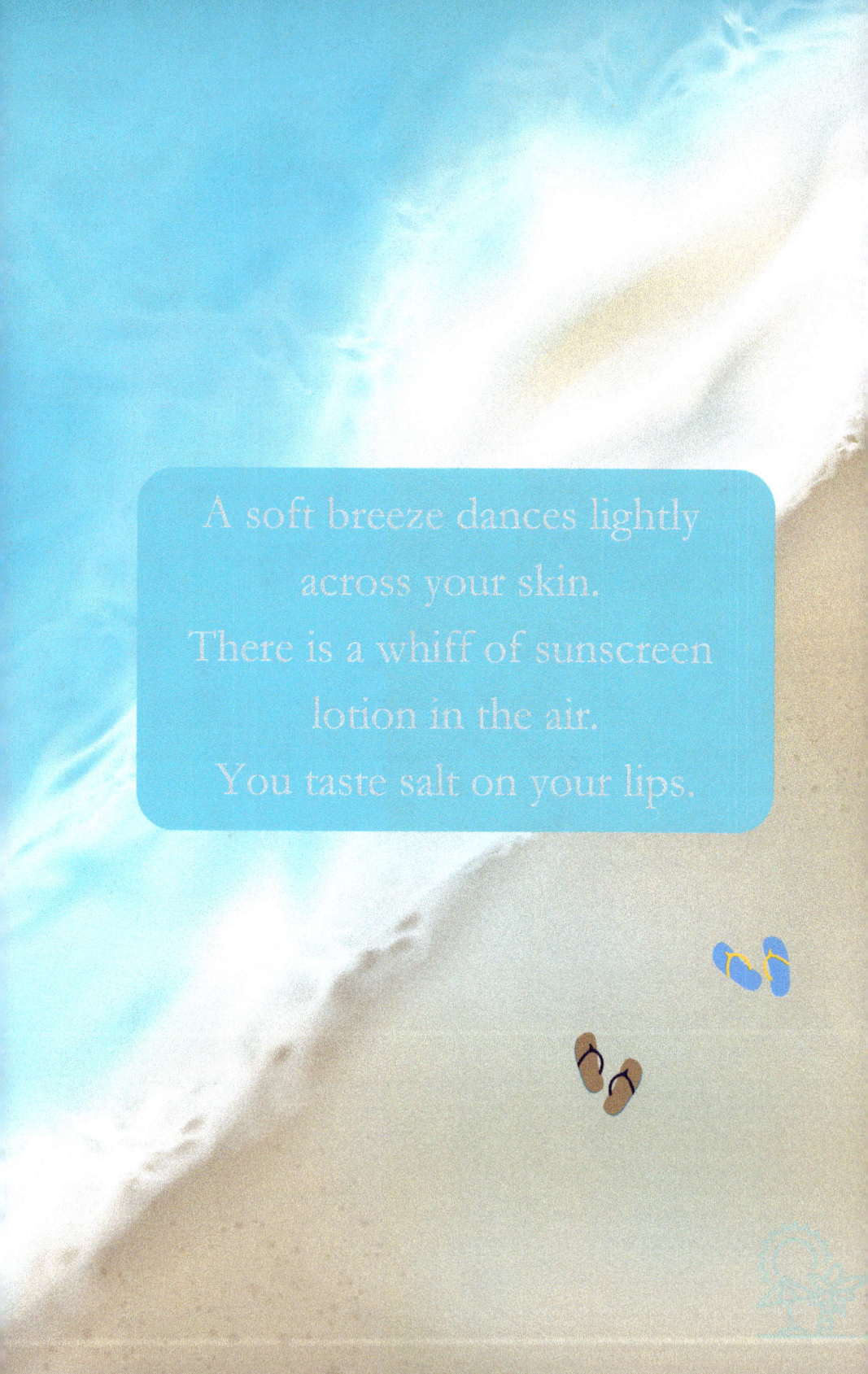

A soft breeze dances lightly across your skin. There is a whiff of sunscreen lotion in the air. You taste salt on your lips.

A few clouds trail peacefully by...

The air is completely still.

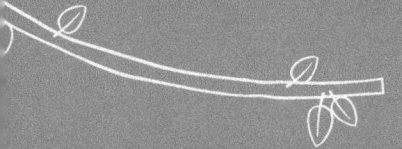

The sky is pure blue and empty.
There are no clouds – no thoughts.

Simply attend to the waves and
nothing else.
The waves crest and roll,
mirroring your inhale and exhale.

You and the ocean breathe as one.

Inhaling as the sea water draws out
into the vast ocean expanse.

Exhaling as the waves roll
back into shore,
foaming and cresting.

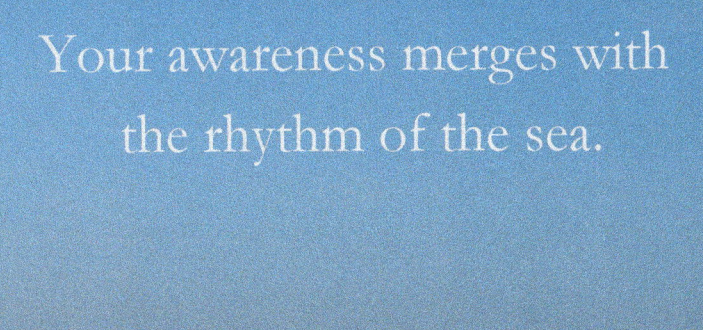

Your awareness merges with the rhythm of the sea.

Visualize deep dark blue ocean depths as you inhale.

Imagine warm, frothy, light blue waves as you exhale.

The waves flow away — taking with them thoughts or emotions you no longer need.

Inhale. Exhale.

The ocean ebbs and flows...

Ebbs and flows.

The warmth of the sun
starts to bring you back
to the outside world.

Peace and tranquility are yours.

Keeping your focus inwards, slowly move your upper body – shoulders, arms, head, and neck.

Twist from side to side.

Gently bring your focus to any
external sounds nearby,
coming back into the day,
fresh, clear, and grounded.

Sit gently within this space until you are ready to resume your day.

As you return to the outside world, know you can tap into this feeling of rest at any time through your day.

Being

Balance & Authenticity

A Visual Meditation Collection

Explore additional visual meditation collections at www.ynqyry.com/Being.

A look inside

Being Happy and Free - Rainbows and Bubbles

Rainbows and Bubbles

Allow this meditation to guide you to a place of deep relaxation and enjoyment, where the playful essence of joy brings renewal, healing and connection.

As you focus on the rain's song, you notice something magical happening.

Imagine yourself wrapped in these colors, the embodiment of all they represent.

Orange representing creativity and joy.

These bubbles represent moments of happiness and freedom in your life.

Keeping your focus inwards, slowly move your upper body
— shoulders, arms, head, and neck.

Twist from side to side

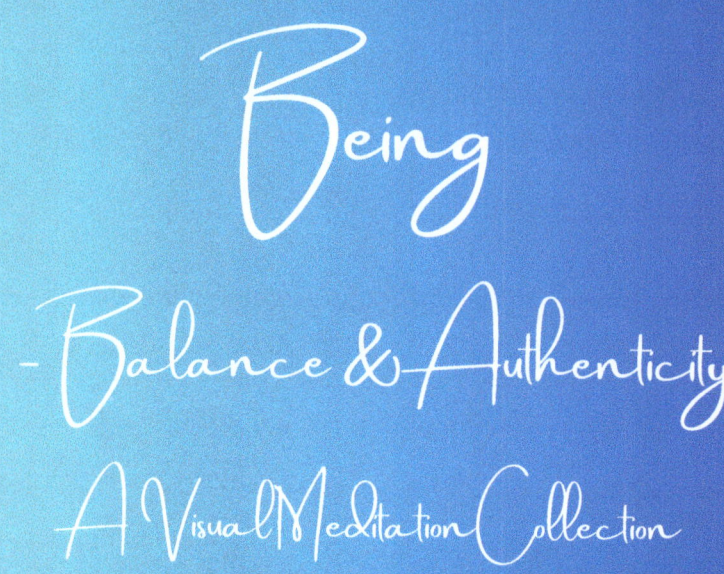

Being

— Balance & Authenticity

A Visual Meditation Collection

SERIES TITLES

BEING RESTFUL
BEING GREEN
BEING JOYFUL
BEING REFRESHED
BEING AWARE
BEING PRESENT
BEING CREATIVE
BEING PEACEFUL
BEING HAPPY AND FREE

Explore additional visual meditation collections at
www.ynqyry.com/Being.

Author Bio

Tanya Clark

Tanya's creative works reflect her own exploration into the power of self-care and mindfulness, and draw on her strengths and experiences to offer practical and heartfelt tools.

A desire to embed balance, authenticity, and peace within the chaos of life drew her deeper into her long-standing yoga practice, and has deeply informed her approach to meditation and relaxation.

Her life story has been a testament to resilience, marked as it has been by personal and professional adversities. These have shaped her understanding of the world, and of the need to ensure there is space in life for pause, reflection, and serenity.

Through meticulously crafted imagery and guided meditations, Tanya invites you to explore these inner landscapes and cultivate a state of calm and inner reflection.

(c) 2024 Tanya Clark
YNQYRY PUBLISHING

www.ingramcontent.com/pod-product-compliance
Lightning Source LLC
Chambersburg PA
CBHW041152110526
44590CB00027B/4207